Imagine 4

WORKBOOK

Daniel Barber

COURSE CONSULTANTS

Elaine Boyd

Paul Dummett

NATIONAL GEOGRAPHIC
LEARNING

Australia • Brazil • Canada • Mexico • Singapore • United Kingdom • United States

National Geographic Learning,
a Cengage Company

***Imagine* 4 Workbook**

Author: Daniel Barber

Course Consultants: Elaine Boyd, Paul Dummett

Publisher: Rachael Gibbon

Executive Editor: Joanna Freer

Project Manager: Natalie Roberts

Lead Editor: Yvonne Molfetas

Editorial Assistant: Polly McLachlan

Director of Global Marketing: Ian Martin

Product Marketing Manager: Fernanda De Oliveira

Heads of Strategic Marketing:

Charlotte Ellis (Europe, Middle East and Africa)

Justin Kaley (Asia and Greater China)

Irina Pereyra (Latin America)

Senior Content Project Manager: Beth McNally

Senior Media Researcher: Leila Hishmeh

Senior Art Director: Brenda Carmichael

Operations Support: Rebecca G. Barbush, Hayley Chwazik-Gee

Manufacturing Manager: Eyvett Davis

Composition: Composure

For permission to use material from this text or product,
submit all requests online at **cengage.com/permissions**
Further permissions questions can be emailed to
permissionrequest@cengage.com

ISBN: 978-0-357-91185-3

National Geographic Learning
Cheriton House, North Way,
Andover, Hampshire, SP10 5BE
United Kingdom

Locate your local office at **international.cengage.com/region**

Visit National Geographic Learning online at **ELTNGL.com**
Visit our corporate website at **www.cengage.com**

Printed in the United Kingdom by Ashford Colour Press Ltd.
Print Number: 02   Print Year: 2024

Imagine **4** WORKBOOK

A **Look.** Find, circle and tick the pictures you can find.

i	s	y	e	p	a	u	q	c	e	a
l	n	y	i	o	b	i	k	e	l	t
i	a	a	h	h	e	l	c	t	e	r
c	k	r	n	a	w	s	u	c	c	g
r	e	i	h	c	h	n	p	o	o	e
o	t	v	p	r	t	o	t	o	a	e
c	z	e	b	r	a	w	a	t	t	e
d	t	r	a	i	n	i	n	j	j	r
e	i	m	a	g	i	n	e	y	t	a
l	e	a	c	l	o	g	s	t	c	s
l	a	r	k	i	t	e	t	i	a	n

B **Listen.** Write the words in the correct list. Then write one more word in each list. 🎧 TR: 0.1

> ~~bus~~ cloudy cold elephant field forest helicopter hippo
> lake lorry monkey motorbike mountain sunny tiger windy

transport	animals	places	weather
bus	_____	_____	_____
_____	_____	_____	_____
_____	_____	_____	_____
_____	_____	_____	_____
_____	_____	_____	_____

C Write questions and answers.

1.

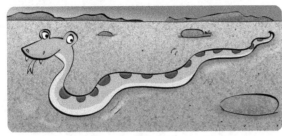

run

_____ Can it run? _____ No, it can't.

4.

play the guitar

_____ _____

2.

swim

_____ _____

5.

see any birds

_____ _____

3.

fly a helicopter

_____ _____

6.

find his glasses

_____ _____

D Complete the sentences about you. Use *always*, *usually*, *sometimes* or *never*.

1. I _____ go shopping at the weekend.

2. I _____ walk to school.

3. I _____ make my bed before I go to school.

4. I _____ read comics with my friends.

5. I _____ play hide-and-seek after school.

6. I _____ make new friends on holiday.

1 Who's Hungry?

A **Write.** Tick the foods that you can see in the picture.

1. m __ lksh __ k __ ☑
2. n __ __ dl __ s ☐
3. p __ nc __ k __ s ☐
4. s __ l __ d ☐

5. s __ ndw __ ch __ s ☐
6. s __ u __ e ☐
7. s __ __ p ☐
8. v __ g __ t __ bl __ s ☐

B **Listen.** Write the food that the children eat. 🎧 TR: 1.1

| burgers | fruit | lemonade | milkshake | pancakes |
| pasta | salad | sandwiches | sauce | water |

1. The girl has some _____ with _____.

2. The boy wants a _____, but he has _____.

3. For breakfast, the girls have _____ with _____ on them.

4. The boys choose _____ and _____.

C **Write about you.**

1. I like eating _____. ☺

2. I don't like eating _____. ☹

A **Write *Is* or *Are*.** Then listen and write the answers. 🎧 TR: 1.2

1. _____Are_____ there any strawberries?   ___Yes, there are.___

2. _____ there a lemon?   _____

3. _____ there any kiwis?   _____

4. _____ there any cheese?   _____

B **Look at the picture on page 6.** Write.

> a   any   lots of   some

1. There's a _____ milkshake.

2. There aren't any _____ noodles.

3. _____ sandwiches.

4. _____ lemonade.

5. _____ chips.

6. _____ orange juice.

C **Write questions about things in your fridge.** Then go to the kitchen and find out!
Answer your questions.

1. Is there any _____ ?

_____

2. Are _____ ?

_____

3. _____ ?

_____

4. _____ ?

_____

A Draw.

1. a bottle
4. a bowl

2. a cup
5. a glass

3. a plate
6. a straw

1.	2.	3.
4.	5.	6.

B Put the lines in the correct order.

a. ... bottles too. This makes lots of plastic ...

b. ... wasting water too! Some restaurants use ...

c. ... lots of plastic: cups, plates, straws and ...

d. ... waste. This plastic often goes into rivers and ...

e. ... seas. It's very bad for wildlife and humans.

f. ... the world's food. So, wasting food is ...

g. Farmers use 70 per cent of the world's water to grow ... 1

C Complete the sentences with *don't* or *always*.

Imagine Restaurant Guide

❶ In a restaurant, _____ ask for more food than you can eat.

❷ _____ ask: 'Can I have a glass of water with no straw, please?'

❸ _____ ask for plastic knives and forks.

❹ Remember to _____ say 'please' when you order something.

❺ Enjoy yourself, but _____ eat at restaurants all the time. It's bad for you and the planet.

A **Put the words in order.**

1. a / can / chicken / have / I / of / please / plate / ?
   Can I have a plate of chicken, please?
   _____

2. please / of / noodles / I / have / can / bowl / a / ?
   _____

3. a / bottle / please / can / have / I / of / water / ?
   _____

4. a / can / have / I / of / pasta / plate / please / ?
   _____

B **Look and write.**

a glass of
orange juice

_____
lemonade

_____
tomato

_____
noodles

_____
sweets

_____
chips

C **Write two things you want to eat or drink now.**

1. I want a _____ of _____.

2. I want _____.

A Say the words with *oo, ue* and *u_e.* Circle the one that doesn't belong. Listen and check. 🎧 TR: 1.3

1.

book computer noodles true

2.

picture ruler June zoo

3.

bedroom Tuesday cube mouse

B Listen. Circle the correct word. 🎧 TR: 1.4

1. cook / cube
2. road / ruler
3. zoo / zone

4. moon / mouse
5. blue / balloon
6. flute / flood

C Look at the pictures and complete the crossword.

Across →

1.
2.
3.

Down ↓

4.
5.
6.

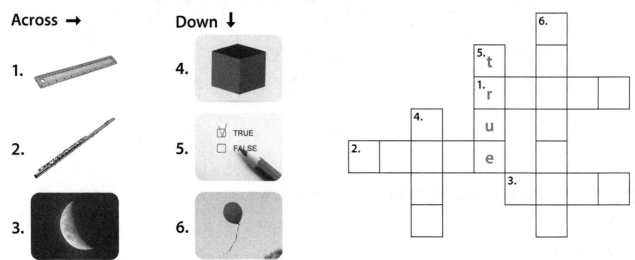

VALUE
Try new things.

A **Which children are trying new things?** Look and tick.

OUR FOOD DIARY	Monday	Tuesday	Wednesday	Thursday	Friday
Carlos ☐	pasta	noodles	pasta	noodles	pasta
Will ☐	cheese sandwich	pancakes	soup	salad	egg sandwich
Mia ☐	burger	pancakes and fruit	soup and salad	pasta	noodles
Anna ☐	burger and salad	burger and salad	burger and water	burger and salad	burger and salad

B **Make a food diary.** Write or draw three new things you want to try.

MY FOOD DIARY	Monday	Tuesday	Wednesday	Thursday	Friday
breakfast					
lunch					
dinner					

2 Animal Life

A **Listen.** Write the animal. There are two animals you don't need. 🎧 TR: 2.1

> ant   bat   kangaroo   panda   parrot   penguin   shark   whale

1. _____ant_____   2. _____   3. _____

4. _____   5. _____   6. _____

B Write.

1. This is a _____dolphin_____.

4. This is a _____.

2. This is a _____.

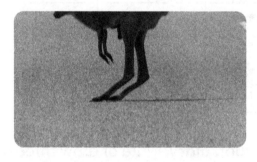

5. This is a _____.

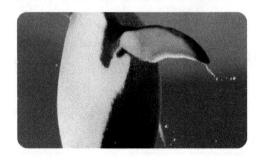

3. This is a _____.

6. This is a _____.

A **Listen and draw lines.** 🎧 TR: 2.2

Arthur   Bill   David

Liam   Lucy   Kim

B **Write.**

1. Carl ___isn't drawing___ (draw) a picture of a monkey. (✗)

   He ___'s taking___ (take) a photo of a monkey. (✓)

2. Fabia _____ (read) about horses. (✓)

   She _____ (learn) about elephants. (✗)

3. The children _____ (give) food to the cat. (✗)

   They _____ (play) with the cat. (✓)

C **Look around the room / your home.** What are you doing? What are other people doing? What aren't you doing? Write three sentences.

_____

_____

_____

A Write. busy lizards safe waking up

1. I'm _____ . I've got lots of work to do.

2. It's eight o' clock in the morning. Are you _____ ?

3. It isn't _____ to play football here because there are lots of cars.

4. Snakes, crocodiles and _____ are all reptiles.

B Write a–g.

It's six o'clock in the morning in Botswana, and the sun is coming up. __b__ But look! What are they doing? _____ It is cold at night, so it's important to warm up.

It's nine o'clock. These meerkats are busy. What are they doing now? _____ They're hungry. But they aren't all looking for food. _____ It's looking for dangerous animals.

It's ten o'clock. _____ There's an eagle! Quick! Hide in the burrow. They are safe there.

It's three o'clock in the afternoon. _____

Now it's eight o'clock. _____ They are safe.

a. One meerkat is climbing a tree.

b. ~~A family of meerkats is waking up.~~

c. Why are they running?

d. They're looking for lizards, small birds, insects or fruit to eat.

e. The meerkats are relaxing and playing in the sun.

f. The meerkats are sleeping in their burrow.

g. They're standing in the sunshine.

C Answer the questions. Write.

1. Why are they standing in the sunshine? _____

2. Why are they looking for lizards, birds, insects and fruit? _____

3. Why is a meerkat climbing a tree? _____

A **Read the answers.** Write the questions.

1. Are you playing the piano?

No, I'm not.

play the piano

3. _____

Yes, she is.

listen to music

2. _____

She's going to the playground.

go

4. _____

Because I'm watching these funny cats. Look!

smile

B **Write questions.**

1. dog / play / ?   Is the dog playing? _____

2. what / birds / do / ?   What are the birds doing? _____

3. what / parrot / say / ?   _____

4. bees / fly / ?   _____

C **Listen.** Answer the questions in Activity B. Write. 🎧 TR: 2.3

1. No, it isn't. It's sleeping. _____   3. _____

2. They're singing. _____   4. _____

A **Say the words with *f* and *ph*.** Write the words in the correct column.

f	ph
_____	alphabet
_____	_____
_____	_____

B **Listen.** Connect the correct letters for the words you hear. TR: 2.4

1.
dol   phin
         ly

2.
al   phabet
       ive

3.
break   fast
          in

4.
so   fa
       phia

5.
f   un
s

6.
f   ruit
b

C **Look.** Find and circle the words from Activity A. There is one extra word with *ph*.

J	T	U	B	D	Q	E	L	P	E	T	A
V	T	H	R	K	C	P	X	U	P	F	G
P	E	L	E	P	H	A	N	T	Z	M	R
C	C	L	A	N	P	Y	H	Q	G	H	A
Y	F	W	K	Q	C	J	G	A	S	P	S
A	O	J	F	P	I	Y	T	J	Y	F	O
R	D	F	A	T	B	Q	L	F	G	B	F
U	V	I	S	Z	O	H	B	N	J	I	A
J	T	S	T	A	L	P	H	A	B	E	T
L	Z	H	P	H	O	T	O	A	P	D	H
Q	N	C	F	U	N	N	Y	K	T	O	E
G	M	V	X	D	O	L	P	H	I	N	R

VALUE

Be interested in animals.

A **Read and match.**

You can show you are interested in animals by ...

1. reading about them in books and on the Internet. `c`

2. keeping an animal as a pet.

3. going for walks in the countryside to see them.

4. learning about animals at school.

5. taking photos of animals you see.

6. drawing pictures of animals.

7. going to wildlife parks and zoos.

8. watching TV programmes about nature.

B **Write three questions about animals.** Then write how you can find the answers. Use the ideas in Activity A.

_____

_____

_____

A **Read about Juan.** What does Juan say to his friend Silvia? Write *So do I* or *Neither do I*.

Juan loves food. He likes going to restaurants. He likes most things. He eats lots of meat, but he never eats fish or eggs. His favourite fruit is watermelon, but he loves all kinds of fruit. He often eats carrots, but he doesn't like other vegetables.

Silvia says:

Juan says:

1. I love food.   So do I.

2. I like restaurants.   _____

3. I don't like fish.   _____

4. I don't eat eggs.   _____

5. I like oranges and mango.   _____

6. I don't like peas.   _____

B **Listen.** Write a tick or a cross. TR: 2.5

1. Do Frida and Abi like chocolate ice cream?   ✓

2. Do Will and Vinny walk to school?   ☐

3. Do Naomi and Frida like baking?   ☐

4. Do Vinny and Abi like roller-skating?   ☐

5. Do Olga and Abi like playing computer games?   ☐

C **Write *So do I* or *Neither do I*.**

1. Paulo likes football.   _____

2. Pasha doesn't eat onions.   _____

3. Oriol and Jaume enjoy playing games.   _____

4. Nadia doesn't like watching TV.   _____

5. Hyung-Jai likes going running.   _____

6. We love ice cream.   _____

D **What do you like?** What don't you like? Write.

1. _____

2. _____

A **Remember the video.** Tick the things that you saw in the video.

B **Do the crossword.**

1. Small fish and whales eat these very small animals.

2. & 5. This big animal eats penguins!

3. Animals eat plants, and other animals eat those animals, etc. This is a _____ .

4. All plants and animals need this. Plants get it from the sun; animals get it from food.

C **Imagine you are in Antarctica.** Write an email to your friends at home. Answer the questions.

> What are you doing?   What can you see?   What's your favourite thing?

Hi _____ ,

I'm in Antarctica! _____

_____

_____

_____

From,

_____

A **Find the words and circle.** Write the words in the table.

unparrotapancakesemblantspastakekangaroofruisaladdinbattysandwichestwhalerisouph

food	animals
	parrot

B **Write the correct word.** There are two words you don't need.

> bat   dolphins   milkshakes   noodles   panda
> penguins   sauce   shark   soup   vegetables

1. These drinks can be chocolate, strawberry or vanilla. _____

2. These friendly animals live in the sea, but they aren't fish. They are usually grey and they always smile. _____

3. This food looks like spaghetti, but it isn't from Italy. _____

4. This big animal is black and white. It eats bamboo. _____

5. These plants are usually green. They are very good for you. _____

6. This big fish has got lots of teeth. Some people think it's scary. _____

7. I like to put this on my burger and chips. _____

8. These birds can't fly, but they can swim very well. _____

C **Read and circle.**

1. There's **a** / **some** banana in the fruit bowl.

2. **Is** / **Are** there any cheese in that sandwich?

3. There are **any** / **lots of** bottles of water in the fridge.

4. There **isn't** / **aren't** any chips on this plate.

5. Can I have a **slice** / **glass** of cake, please?

6. Are there **any** / **some** potatoes in the kitchen?

D **Write questions and answers.**

you / eat / lunch / now / ?

Are you eating
lunch now?
Yes, we are.

where / they / go / ?

what / she / do / ?

he / wash / the dishes / ?

E **Listen to the words with the same sound.** Tick the photo of the word with a different spelling. Write the word. 🎧 TR: 2.6

1. **f** / **ph** The different word is __photo__ .

3. **oo** / **u_e** The different word is _____ .

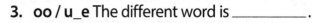

    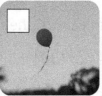 

2. **f** / **ph** The different word is _____ .

4. **oo** / **ue** The different word is _____ .

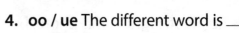

3 Look at Me

A **Listen.** Look and match. 🎧TR: 3.1

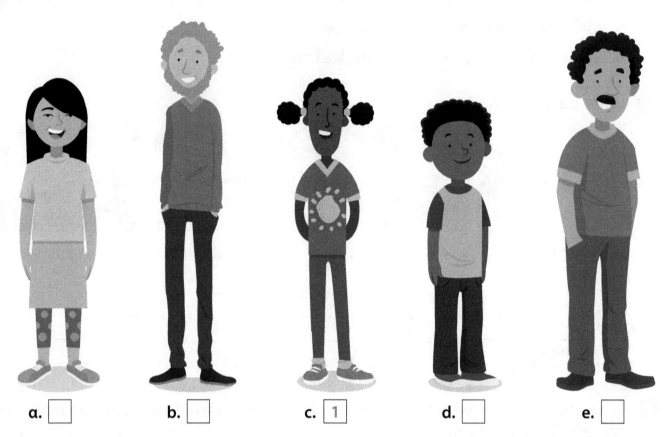

a. ☐   b. ☐   c. 1   d. ☐   e. ☐

B **Write the opposite of the word in bold.**

1. My sister and I are different. Her face is **long**, and my face is ___round___ .

2. She isn't **short**, she's very _____ !

3. You're not **fat**! I think you're _____ .

4. Kera has got **dark** hair, but Noreen's hair is _____ .

5. His hair is **straight** in this photo, but in that photo it's _____ .

C **Write about you.** Describe yourself.

1. I'm _____ .

2. I've got _____ .

22

A **Look and circle.**

Patty   Anna   Roshni

1. Roshni is taller than **Anna** / (**Patty**) / **Anna and Patty**.

2. Anna has got straighter hair than **Patty** / **Roshni** / **Patty and Roshni**.

3. Patty's hair is darker than **Anna's** / **Roshni's** / **Anna's and Roshni's** hair.

4. Anna's hair is shorter than **Patty's** / **Roshni's** / **Patty's and Roshni's** hair.

5. Patty's face is rounder than **Anna's** / **Roshni's** / **Anna's and Roshni's** faces.

B **Look and write.**

1. Anna / tall / Roshni   Anna is taller than Roshni._____

2. Roshni / straight / hair / Patty   _____

3. Anna / light / hair / Roshni   _____

4. Patty's hair / long / Anna's hair   _____

C **Write true sentences about you and your family.**

1. My brother is taller than me._____

2. _____

3. _____

A **Put the letters in order.**

The man with the longest beard is from India. Sarwan Singh's beard is

1._____ (**stomla**) 2.5 2._____ (**mstree**) long. But his beard isn't the

longest beard in history. Hans Langseth lived in the US. His beard was 5.33 metres

long when he 3._____ (**dide**) in 1927!

Interesting fact: it usually 4._____ (**tskea**) nine months for a beard to grow

10 centimetres.

B **Read and write.**

~~long~~	long	long	old
short	takes	tall	tall

Is your hair 1._____long_____? Yes? But it's

shorter than Xie Qiuping's hair. She's from

China, and her hair is 5.6 metres long! She's

got the 2._____est hair in the

world. There's a man in India who has got

the 3._____est moustache in the world. Ram Singh Chauhan's moustache is longer

than 4 metres! Ram says it 4._____ two hours to wash his moustache every day.

Sultan Kösen is from Turkey. He's the 5._____est person in the world. He's 251

centimetres tall! He's also got the biggest hands! The world's 6._____est man,

Edward Niño Hernández from Colombia, is only 72 centimetres 7._____!

And the 8._____est person? Jeanne Calment was 122 years old when she died in

1997. Almost all of the oldest people are women.

C **Read again.** Write T (true) or F (false).

1. Xie Qiuping has got the longest hair in the world. _____

2. Ram Singh Chauhan is the tallest person in the world. _____

3. Sultan Kösen is the shortest man in the world. _____

4. Edward Niño Hernández has got the longest moustache in the world. _____

5. Jeanne Calment was the oldest person in the world. _____

A **Look.** Write T (true) or F (false).

Year: 2021
Speed: 80 km/h

Year: 2003
Speed: 200 km/h

Year: 1970
Speed: 50 km/h

1. The Twimby is newer than the Rocket. _____

2. The oldest car is the Rocket. _____

3. The Tank is slower than the Rocket. _____

4. The fastest car is the Twimby. _____

5. The Tank is bigger than the Rocket. _____

6. The Twimby is the smallest car. _____

B **Listen and write.** 🎧 TR: 3.2

1. short / tall

   Fabio is the ___tallest___ .

   Benny is the _____ .

2. dark / light

   Tess has got the _____ hair.

   Maria has got the _____ hair.

3. big / small

   Lenny's pencil case is the _____ .

   Klara's pencil case is the _____ .

4. old / young

   Benedict is the _____ .

   Victor is the _____ .

C **Write sentences about the students in your class.**

1. big / small school bag _____

2. dark / light hair _____

3. long / short hair _____

A **Say the words with *ir, or* and *ar*.** Circle the one that doesn't belong. Write the word. Listen and check. 🎧 TR: 3.3

1. ir _____shorts_____

3. ar _____

2. or _____

4. ir _____

B **Listen.** Circle the correct letters for the words you hear. 🎧 TR: 3.4

1. ir / or

2. ir / ar

3. ar / or

4. ir / or / ar

5. ir / or / ar

6. ir / or / ar

C **Look.** Match the puzzle pieces to make a word.

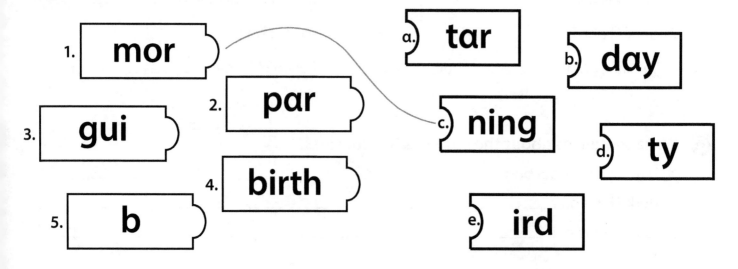

1. mor
2. par
3. gui
4. birth
5. b

a. tar
b. day
c. ning
d. ty
e. ird

VALUE

Accept differences.

A **Which children are accepting differences?** Look and tick.

1. ☐

3. ☐

2. ☐

4. ☐

B **What about you?** Read and circle. 1 = This is never true; 5 = This is always true.

1. I'm happy to play games with children who play differently.   1 2 3 4 5

2. I'm friendly to children who look different from me.   1 2 3 4 5

3. I'm interested in children's hobbies that are different from mine.   1 2 3 4 5

4. I like making friends with people who speak other languages.   1 2 3 4 5

5. I'm happy to play with children who wear different clothes from me.   1 2 3 4 5

Lesson 1 Vocabulary

A Look and circle.

 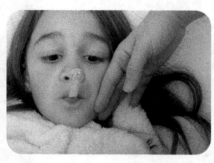 

1. He has got **a sore shoulder** / **stomach ache**.

2. She **has got a cough** / **is ill**.

3. He has got **a cold** / **toothache**.

4. She has got a **cough** / **sore neck**.

5. He has got a **cold** / **sore shoulder**.

6. She has got **a sore neck** / **backache**.

B Listen and write. 🎧 TR: 4.1

1. The woman has got _____ .

2. The boy has got _____ .

3. The girl has got a _____ .

4. The girl takes some _____ .

5. The man has got _____ .

C Write parts of the body.

I've got

_____ ache.

_____ ache.

_____ ache.

a sore _____ .

A Write *must* or *mustn't*.

1. **A:** I've got a sore shoulder.

   B: You _____ play tennis for a few days.

2. **A:** Johann is ill.

   B: Why is he at school? He _____ go home and go to bed.

3. **A:** I've got toothache.

   B: You _____ eat any more sweets, then.

4. **A:** We're home! Is it lunchtime?

   B: Yes. You _____ wash your hands before you eat.

B Write *must* or *mustn't* and a verb from the box.

climb   have   run   wear

1.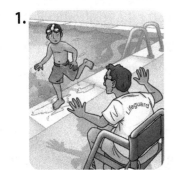
   Hey! You
   _____!

2.
   Excuse me, you
   _____
   a life jacket.

3.
   Hey! You
   _____
   up there.

4.
   Stop! You
   _____
   a shower before
   you come in.

C Write three school rules. Use *must* and *mustn't*.

must	mustn't
1. You must listen to the teacher.	3.
2.	4.

A Write.

| calm grades worry |

Yoga helps children at Bronxville Elementary School to be 1._____ . They learn not to 2._____ or get angry, and it helps them get good 3._____ in exams.

B Read and write.

| at home easy to do in the morning |
| it's good learn at school not to worry or just two |

It isn't always easy to 1._____ . When do you learn well? First thing 2._____ ? After you play in the playground?

Children at Bronxville Elementary School in the US do yoga. They say it's fantastic. It helps them to be calm and 3._____ or get angry. When they are calm, the children get good grades in exams. They say 4._____ to do yoga because they can study and learn better.

Next time you want to learn well at school or study well 5._____ , try yoga! It's quick and 6._____ . You can do it in the playground or in your classroom, sitting at your desk! You can do it in 15 minutes ... 7._____ ! Go on! Give it a go!

C Read again. Circle the correct answer.

1. At school, it's:
   a. always easy to learn.
   b. never easy to learn.
   c. sometimes difficult to learn.

2. Children at Bronxville Elementary School:
   a. don't like doing yoga.
   b. think yoga is fantastic.
   c. feel angry after yoga.

3. Yoga is good because:
   a. it is a fun sport.
   b. the teacher is calm.
   c. it helps children study and learn.

4. Yoga is:
   a. quick to do.
   b. difficult to start.
   c. beautiful to watch.

A **Read and circle.**

1. It **is** / **isn't** healthy to watch TV all day.

2. It **is** / **isn't** important to brush your teeth before you go to bed.

3. It **is lots of** / **isn't much** fun to climb trees with your friends.

4. It **is** / **isn't** nice to say bad words to people.

5. It **is** / **isn't** good to wear a jacket when it's hot and sunny.

6. It **is** / **isn't** friendly to say 'Hello' to people in the street.

B **Listen.** Do the people think the sentences in Activity A are true? Write a tick or a cross.

🎧 TR: 4.2

1. ✓   2. ☐   3. ☐   4. ☐   5. ☐   6. ☐

C **Look and write.**

1. nice / ice cream / on hot, sunny days

_____

3. healthy / some exercise / every day

_____

2. fun / to school / with no friends

_____

4. important / win all the time

_____

A **Say the words with *ou* and *ow*.** Circle the one that doesn't belong. Listen and check. 🎧 TR: 4.3

1. mouse   cloud   window   shower
2. town   mountain   soup   towel
3. playground   loud   cow   rainbow

B **Listen.** Circle the correct word. 🎧 TR: 4.4

1. shower / skirt
2. mouse / monkey
3. house / horse
4. barn / bounce
5. cow / coat
6. dark / down

C **Look at the pictures and complete the crossword.**

Across →

 1.

 2.

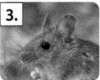 3.

Down ↓

 4.

 5.

 6.

2. s

VALUE

Stay in shape.

A Write the activities in the correct column.

baking	collecting stickers	playing computer games	playing football
playing tennis	reading	riding your bike	running
swimming	walking	watching TV	

Stay in shape with these activities	Don't stay in shape with these activities

B How do you stay in shape? Write about you.

1. _____
2. _____
3. _____
4. _____
5. _____
6. _____

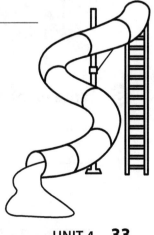

A Do the crossword.

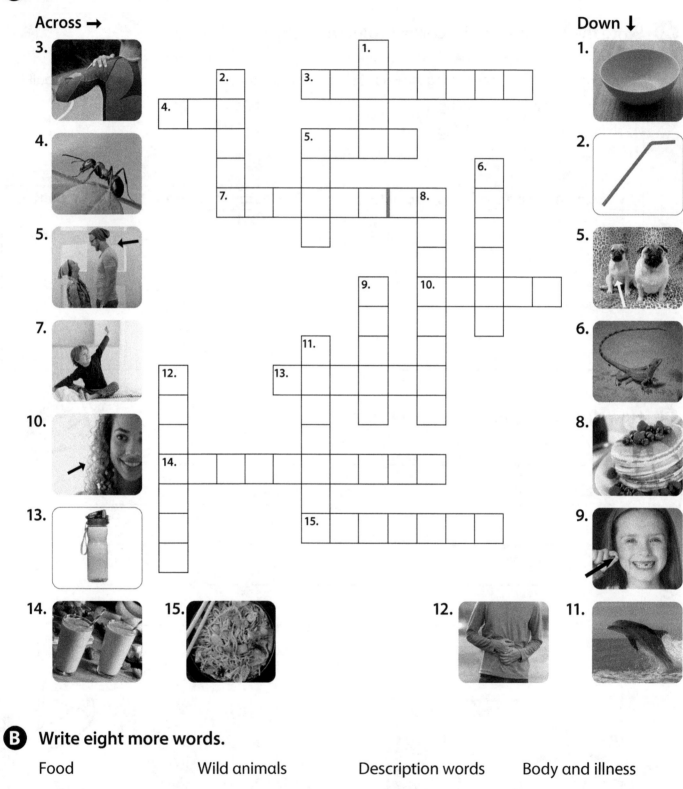

Across →

Down ↓

B Write eight more words.

Food	Wild animals	Description words	Body and illness
_____	_____	_____	_____
_____	_____	_____	_____

Solar Eclipses

A **Listen.** Tick the words you hear. 🎧 TR: 4.5

always ☐	glasses ☐	often ☐
cold ☐	hat ☐	safe ☐
darker ☐	hours ☐	sun ☐
easy ☐	minutes ☐	two ☐
four ☐	moon ☐	

B **Complete the summary with the words you ticked in Activity A.**

Solar eclipses happen when the [1]_____ goes behind the [2]_____ .
This makes it [3]_____ during the day, but only for a few [4]_____ .
Eclipses don't happen very [5]_____ . A place on earth gets an eclipse once
every [6]_____ hundred years. Be careful, because looking at the sun isn't
[7]_____ . You must wear special [8]_____ or make a 'pinhole viewer'.

C **Label the diagram.** | eclipse here   the earth   the moon   the sun |

_____   _____   **SOLAR ECLIPSE**

_____   _____

D **Tick the questions that the text in your Student's Book answers.**

1. What is a solar eclipse? ☐
2. What happens on earth when there is a solar eclipse? ☐
3. When is the next eclipse? ☐
4. How often do solar eclipses happen? ☐
5. Where is a good place to see an eclipse? ☐
6. What is a safe way to see an eclipse? ☐

A **Cross out the word that doesn't belong.**

1. curly   long   ~~tall~~   straight
2. cold   cough   medicine   toothache
3. back   beard   hair   moustache
4. dark   fat   short   tall
5. back   neck   shoulder   teeth

B **Listen, colour and write.** There is one example. 🎧 TR: 4.6

C **Write.**

1. Lions are _____ (small) than elephants.

2. Elephants are the _____ (big) animals in Africa.

3. Giraffes are _____ and _____ (tall, thin) than hippos.

4. Snakes are _____ (long) than frogs.

D **Write sentences.**

1. fun / ride bike / with friends

   It's fun to ride your bike with friends.

2. mustn't / roller-skate / in the house

   You mustn't roller-skate in the house.

3. important / drink water / in hot weather

4. healthy / go to school / by bike

5. must / tell / parents / before / go outside

6. not safe / ride bike / on a busy street

7. must / stop / when the light is red

8. not safe / ride bike / in the dark / with no lights

E **Circle the two words that have got the same vowel sound.**
Listen and check. TR: 4.7

1. (around) (now) short window

2. birthday mouse skirt through

3. car hair park panda

4. flower young show cloud

5. morning shout start transport

6. above cow father playground

5 I Love My Town

A **Put the letters in order.** Tick the places that you can see in the picture.

1. apishlot _____hospital_____ ✓

2. orpsst recent _____ ☐

3. parketmuser _____ ☐

4. amenci _____ ☐

5. féac _____ ☐

6. trekam _____ ☐

7. sub pots _____ ☐

8. arc karp _____ ☐

B **Listen and write.** What is it? 🎧 TR: 5.1

1. _____car park_____

2. _____

3. _____

4. _____

5. _____

6. _____

7. _____

8. _____

A Look at the picture on p. 38. Write *was*, *were*, *wasn't* or *weren't*.

A: In the 1950s, 1._____was_____ there a hospital in the town?

B: Yes, there 2._____ , but it 3._____ smaller than the hospital we've got now.

A: And 4._____ there any cinemas?

B: Yes, there 5._____ . But there 6._____ a sports centre.

A: 7._____ there a café?

B: Yes, there 8._____ a nice café. There 9._____ any big supermarkets.

B Look and write about a town in 1990.

(✓)

SHOP

1. __There was a shop.__
   _____

(✗)

2. __There weren't any__
   __bus stops.__

(✗)

CINEMA

3. _____
   _____

(✓)

SUPERMARKET

4. _____
   _____

(✓)

Café   Café

5. _____
   _____

(✗)

6. _____
   _____

C Ask someone in your family about your town in 1990. Write the answers.

1. __Were there any shops__ ?   __Yes, there were__ .

2. _____ ?   _____ .

3. _____ ?   _____ .

4. _____ ?   _____ .

A **Write the words.**

1. s_____   2. f_____   3. s_____

   c_____

B **Read.** Write a–e.

A megacity is a city with more than 10 million people. In 2020, there were 34 megacities in the world. 1._____ where many cities are getting bigger and bigger. 2._____

This is Shenzhen. 3._____ But about 40 years ago, it was very different. In those days, it was a small fishing town with only 59,000 people. But then, the big companies arrived. 4._____ These factories make things like tablets and smartphones. Shenzhen now has one the largest electronics markets in the world.

5._____ These days, about 12 million people live in and around Shenzhen. Where do you live? How is it the same as Shenzhen? How is it different?

a. It's a very big city in China.

b. Seven of them were in China,

c. There are huge supermarkets and shopping centres here too.

d. And the skyscrapers are getting taller and taller!

e. Very soon, there were big factories and many new jobs for people.

C **Read again.** Circle the correct word.

1. Megacities have got more than ten **thousand / million / billion** people.

2. There were **seven / sixteen / thirty-four** megacities in China in 2020.

3. In China, many **people / electronics / skyscrapers** are getting taller and taller.

4. In 1980, Shenzhen was **much smaller / the same size / much bigger** than today.

A **Write the expressions in the correct column.**

> 60 years ago   in those days   now   then   these days

Today	In the past

B **Listen to Olivia and her grandad.** Write. 🎧 TR: 5.2

1. Olivia's grandad was _____ years old about 60 years ago, in 1962.

2. In those days, there weren't any _____ .

3. There were _____ then, but there wasn't one in Olivia's grandad's _____ .

4. These days we can watch films at _____ all the time.

5. But 60 years ago, the only films were at the _____ .

C **Read and write.**

> ago   days   now   then   these

Seventy years ¹·_____ , Tokyo and New York City were the first megacities in the world. In those ²·_____ , skyscrapers were a new type of building in many cities around the world, and the tallest skyscrapers in the world were in New York. The tallest building ³·_____ was the Empire State Building, at 381 metres. ⁴·_____ days, the tallest buildings in the world are mostly in Asia and the Middle East. The Burj Khalifa in the UAE is almost 830 metres tall! ⁵·_____ , they are building taller buildings in other cities.

A Say the words with *ir, ur, or* and *er.* Circle the one that doesn't belong. Listen and check. 🎧 TR: 5.3

1. curly   world   thirsty   car

2. person   story   burger   skirt

3. shirt   word   chair   bird

B Listen. Circle the correct word. 🎧 TR: 5.4

1. dirty / party
2. burger / beard
3. door / world

4. parrot / purple
5. third / turn
6. forest / far

C Look. Match the puzzle pieces to make a word.

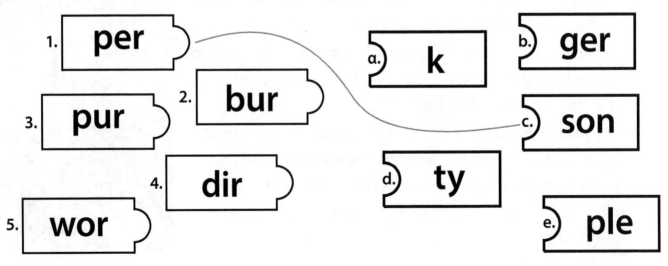

1. per
2. bur
3. pur
4. dir
5. wor

a. k
b. ger
c. son
d. ty
e. ple

VALUE

Love your town.

A **Which children love their town?** Look and circle.

B **How do you love your town?** Tick the things you do now. Underline the things you can do. Write one more idea.

1. I always throw my rubbish away. ☐

2. I am a member of a local sports club or other club. ☐

3. I help visitors in my town. ☐

4. I volunteer to pick up litter. ☐

5. I clean up the park. ☐

6. Your idea: _____.

6 Yesterday and Long Ago

A Write the words.

1. <u>c</u> <u>r</u> y

2. ___ ___ ___ g ___

3. ___ a i ___

4. ___ e ___ ___
___ a ___ r

5. ___ ___ i t f ___ ___
___ ___ e ___ u ___

6. ___ t ___ y ___ t
h ___ ___ ___

B Listen and write. 🎧 TR: 6.1

1. The girls _____need_____ _____water_____ .

2. James wants to _____ _____ _____ today.

3. Matt says you can _____ _____ at camp.

4. Orla _____ _____ _____ in 15 minutes.

C Write about you.

1. What do you do when your friend tells you a funny joke?

_____

2. What do you do when you see a sad film?

_____

3. How do you get to school?

_____

A Write.

  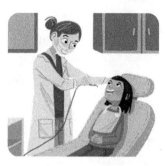

1. He _____ (climb) a mountain two weeks ago.

   He _____ (not / wait) for his friend.

2. He _____ (not / walk) to school yesterday.

   He _____ (cycle) to school with a friend.

3. She _____ (need) to go to the dentist after school last Monday.

   She _____ (not / cry).

B Write the verbs in the past simple.

> dance   live   not stay   not write   paint   play   ~~sail~~   travel   use

New Zealand is a country in the Pacific Ocean. Before people from Europe ¹._____**sailed**_____ to New Zealand, many people already ²._____ there. They were the Māori people. The Māori ³._____ amazing boats to go from place to place in New Zealand. Some Māori people ⁴._____ in New Zealand. They ⁵._____ from New Zealand to live in the Chatham Islands – 800 kilometres away!

The Māori people speak their own language, and they are good storytellers. They ⁶._____ stories in books. They ⁷._____ music with instruments made from sea shells and ⁸._____ special dances called the *haka*, the *poi* and the *whakawatea*. They ⁹._____ their faces with shapes called *moko*.

C Write the last time you did these things. Use *ago, last* or *yesterday*.

1. walk to school   I walked to school yesterday.

2. climb a tree   _____

3. laugh   _____

4. cry   _____

5. dance   _____

A Write.

> civilisations invented mystery statues

1. Artists usually make _____ of famous or important people.

2. It's a _____ how people built huge buildings many years ago.

3. The Egyptians, Aztecs and Maya were all successful, old _____ .

4. Who _____ toothpaste? I think it was the ancient Egyptians.

B Read. Write a–d.

Ancient Egyptians didn't write down their history, so many things about this time are a mystery.

One of the mysteries is the Great Sphinx of Giza. 1._____ It's got the head of a man and the body of a lion! It is 20 metres tall. 2._____ No, they didn't. Most people think it took 100 men three years to make the statue. 3._____ or why they made it. 4._____ One thing is for sure: it didn't look like it does today!

a. Nobody knows for sure exactly how old it is,

b. What it looked like long ago is also a mystery.

c. It is one of the oldest and largest statues in the world.

d. Did they make it with machines?

C Write.

1. The Ancient Egyptians didn't write down their _____ .

2. The Great Sphinx of Giza has got the _____ of a man and the _____ of a lion.

3. Many believe it took 100 _____ three _____ to make the statue.

4. The Ancient Egyptians didn't make the statue with _____.

A **Listen.** Circle the correct answer. 🎧 TR: 6.2

1. Did Cary cycle to school?   Yes, he did.   No, he didn't.

2. Did he study English?   Yes, he did.   No, he didn't.

3. Did he stay at home in the afternoon?   Yes, he did.   No, he didn't.

4. Did he and his friend play computer games?   Yes, they did.   No, they didn't.

5. Did Cary's sister play the piano?   Yes, she did.   No, she didn't.

6. Did he and his dad watch a film?   Yes, they did.   No, they didn't.

B **Look at the photos.** Write questions and answers.

1. he / practise / guitar / on Saturday
   Did he practise guitar on Saturday _____ ?

   No, he didn't _____ .

2. they / cycle / in the park / this morning
   _____ ?

   _____ .

3. she / bake / with her mum / last weekend
   _____ ?

   _____ .

4. they / play / hide-and-seek / at school
   _____ ?

   _____ .

C **Write three questions to ask a person in your family about what he or she did yesterday.** Ask the questions and write a tick or a cross.

1. Did you laugh at a film yesterday? _____ X ___

2. _____ _____

3. _____ _____

4. _____ _____

A **Listen.** Write the words. Then write the words in the correct column. 🎧 TR: 6.3

1. b <u>e</u> <u>a</u> <u>r</u>   2. h__ __ __   3. p__ __ __   4. st__ __ __s

5. ch__ __ __   6. p__ __ ents   7. squ__ __ __   8. w__ __ __

air	ear	are	ar
_____	__bear__	_____	_____
_____	_____		
_____	_____		

B **Listen.** Circle the correct word. 🎧 TR: 6.4

1. bar / (bear)

2. score / square / scare

3. hair / her / hear

4. wore / wear

5. grandparents / parents / presents

6. tear / turn / tore

C **Read the clues.** Find and circle the words.

F	U	N	F	A	I	R	S	S	N	X	M
N	F	K	J	W	G	V	X	Y	S	W	D
C	L	G	S	S	R	T	F	R	E	R	S
G	X	N	Q	C	A	E	S	C	J	T	X
V	S	V	U	A	N	A	W	S	P	R	W
A	R	P	A	R	D	R	P	G	E	P	E
J	U	C	R	E	P	Q	Q	V	A	X	A
T	L	F	E	G	A	C	N	T	R	E	R
N	X	H	A	I	R	H	F	N	W	M	I
D	I	T	D	I	E	A	V	X	N	J	N
E	H	T	C	R	N	I	Z	T	W	A	G
G	O	H	A	Q	T	R	J	D	D	B	F

Words with *air*
1. It's on your head.
2. You can sit on it.
3. A fun place

Words with *ear*
1. You're doing it with your clothes.
2. Delicious green fruit
3. To pull apart

Words with *are*
1. Not a circle
2. To make someone afraid

Words with *ar*
1. Your parent's parent

VALUE

Be interested in others.

A **Match the pictures (1–4) to the expressions (a–f).** You can match more than one expression to each picture.

a. Be interested in people from other countries.

b. Be interested in people from the past.

c. Be interested in people's hobbies.

d. Be interested in people's lives.

e. Be interested in people's problems.

f. Be interested in what people like and don't like.

1. _____

3. _____

2. _____

4. _____

B **Write two ways that you show you are interested in other people.**

1. _____

2. _____

A **Read and tick the suggestions.**

1. Do you want to bake a cake? ☐

2. Let's go to the cinema. ☐

3. No, I don't want to. ☐

4. Should we stop at this café? I'm thirsty. ☐

5. We were at the swimming pool yesterday. ☐

6. Why don't we go for a walk? ☐

B **Listen. Write.** 🎧 TR: 6.5

> I'm not sure   No, I don't want to   Shall we   Why don't we   Yes, let's   Yes, OK

Flávia: Hi! What would you like to do? Would you like to play outside?

Gloria: 1._____ . It's starting to rain.

Flávia: Is it? Oh no! 2._____ go up to my bedroom to play?

Gloria: 3._____ . What games have you got?

Flávia: I've got lots of party clothes. 4._____ dress up?

Gloria: 5._____ . I don't like dressing up.

Flávia: Really? OK. What would you like to do?

Gloria: You've got some really good puzzles, haven't you? Let's do a puzzle.

Flávia: 6._____ ! I love doing puzzles! Do you want to try a 500-piece puzzle?

Gloria: Wow! OK.

C **Write responses.** If the response is *no*, say why.

1. Why don't we bike to the park? (✓) That's a good idea!

2. Do you want to play football? (✗) No, I don't want to. I don't like football.

3. Shall we bake a cake? (✓) _____

4. Let's climb trees in the garden. (✗) _____

5. Why don't we draw a picture? (✓) _____

A **Remember the video.** Tick the things that you saw in the video.

B **Match 1–5 to a–e to make sentences about the Pueblo people.**

1. Pueblo people are ___

2. Their ancestors were here ___

3. There are 21 pueblos where the Pueblo people live. 'Pueblo' ___

4. The Puebloans make their buildings by using a mixture of water, ___

5. They keep many of the old traditions, like ___

a. mud and straw.

b. means 'village'.

c. many years ago.

d. getting water from a river and using brick ovens.

e. from Texas, Arizona and New Mexico in the US.

C **Imagine it is the year 1400 and you are in Taos Pueblo.** Write about the things you can see. Use the questions to help you.

What time of day is it? What can you see? Describe the village. What are the people doing? Talk about two people you can see. Listen. What sounds can you hear? Is anyone cooking? Are there any animals?

I'm here in Taos Pueblo in New Mexico. It is the year 1400. _____

_____

_____

_____

A **Look and write.** Find and write the extra word.

1.

2.

3.

4.

5.

6.

7.

8.

Extra word: ______________

B **Write two words in each sentence.**

~~cycles + centre~~ café + needed
cry + climbed wait + stop

1. She ___cycles___ past the sports ___centre___ on her way to school.
2. You must ______________ for the number 12 bus at the bus ______________ across the street.
3. He didn't ______________ when he ______________ the tree and hurt his arm.
4. They stopped at the ______________ because they ______________ water.

C **Write the verbs in the past simple.**

1. He _____learnt_____ (learn) English when he _____ (live) in the US.

2. His granddad _____ (not / use) computers until he _____ (be) 72!

3. She _____ (want) to play computer games, but she _____ (need) to do her homework first.

4. There _____ (not / be) any buses so she _____ (walk) home.

5. She _____ (stay) at home because she _____ (be) ill.

6. We _____ (watch) a sad film, but I _____ (not / cry).

D **Write the answers.**

1. Did she find her bag?   Yes, _____she did_____ .

2. Were there any people in the restaurant?   No, _____ .

3. Did they finish the project?   No, _____ .

4. Did you like the film?   No, _____ .

5. Was there a boy with curly hair at the library?   Yes, _____ .

6. Did you and your brother bake that cake?   Yes, _____ .

E **Circle the two words that have got the same vowel sound.** Listen and check. 🎧 TR: 6.6

1. (girl)   sports   (word)

2. pear   fair   year

3. square   wear   beard

4. curly   Thursday   four

5. here   work   were

6. chair   near   parents

7 The Great Outdoors

A **Look.** Write the words.

1. <u>l o s e</u> your w<u>a</u> <u>y</u>

2. s_ _ _ _ i_ a l_ _ _ _

3. h_ _ _ a p_ _ _ _ _ _

4. g_ c_ _ _ _ _ _ _ _ _

5. s_ _ _ _ _ i_ a t_ _ _ _

6. s_ _ _ a s_ _ _ _ _ _ _ _ _ s_ _ _

B **Listen.** Answer the questions. Write a tick or a cross. 🎧 TR: 7.1

1. Did Matt enjoy his school trip? ✓

4. Did they eat outside? ☐

2. Did he make friends? ☐

5. Did they go canoeing? ☐

3. Did they sleep outside? ☐

6. Did they swim in the lake? ☐

C Write two things you want to do outdoors.

1. I want to _____.

2. _____

A **Find ten verbs in the past simple.** Write them in the present simple and past simple.

w	r	o	d	e	g	s
e	s	w	a	m	o	l
n	a	g	l	a	t	e
t	t	h	a	d	o	p
l	o	s	t	e	n	t
y	s	a	w	t	w	i

1. _____eat_____ _____ate_____

2. _____ _____

3. _____ _____

4. _____ _____

5. _____ _____

6. _____ _____

7. _____ _____

8. _____ _____

9. _____ _____

10. _____ _____

B **Listen and write.** TR: 7.2

Jamil

Yesterday, Jamil ¹·_____ at 9:00. In the morning, he ²·_____ for an hour.
Then he and his family ³·_____ outside in the garden.

Naomi

Last weekend, Naomi ⁴·_____ to the park and ⁵·_____ a picnic.
She ⁶·_____ friends with another girl there.

Bea

Yesterday, Bea went to the cinema, but she ⁷·_____ a film. She ⁸·_____
the money for the film. She ⁹·_____ a good night.

C **Write what you did yesterday.**

1. I slept for eight hours. _____

2. _____

3. _____

A **Label the picture with the words.** explorer ski sled

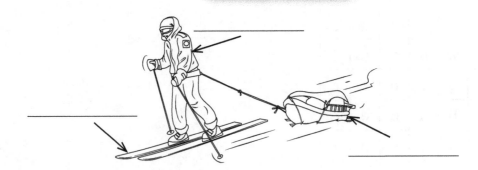

B **Read.** Write a–d.

Meet Jade Hameister. She's from Melbourne in Australia, but in this photo she is a long way from home!

1._____ First, she went to the Arctic. She became the youngest person to ski to the North Pole. She skied more than 150 kilometres in 11 days.

2._____ Yes, very! It was very cold – about -25°C. Her sled was very heavy – 50 kilograms, the same as her! It was very difficult, but she never stopped.

3._____ She went with her dad, Paul. He's an explorer too.

4._____ In April 2016, when she was 14. After that, she skied across Greenland in May 2017, and to the South Pole six months later. She travelled a total of 2,000 kilometres before she was 17!

a. Was it difficult?

b. When did she go on this adventure?

c. Where did she go?

d. Who did she go with?

C **Read again.** Write T (true) or F (false).

1. Jade travelled far from her home. _____

2. She rode in a sled to the North Pole. _____

3. The journey was difficult for more than one reason. _____

4. She went to the North Pole with a friend. _____

A Look. Match the questions (1–6) to the answers (a–f).

1. What did she see?
2. Where did she see it?
3. When did this happen?
4. What did she do?
5. Who did she tell?
6. What did he say?

a. Under the tree in the garden.
b. Her dad.
c. 'I didn't see it.'
d. She took a photo.
e. Last night, before she went to bed.
f. She saw a big animal.

B Write questions and answers. Use *Where, Who, What* and *When*.

1. you / see / at the cinema

   we / a film called *Nine Years*

   <u>What did you see at the cinema?</u>

   <u>We saw a film called *Nine Years*.</u>

2. he / go / on holiday

   he / to South Africa

3. they / sleep / in a tent

   they / last week

4. she / paint / in art class

   she / her sister

C Write questions about the past. Use *What, When* or *Where*.

1. you / TV   <u>What did you watch on TV last night?</u>

2. your dad / breakfast

3. your friends / holiday

A Circle the two words that have got the same sound. Listen and check. 🎧 TR: 7.3

1. centre   girl   pencil   giant
2. canoe   village   giraffe   moustache
3. centre   vegetable   pancake   dangerous
4. page   cough   city   mice
5. huge   change   building   tiger
6. face   stomach   much   bounce

B Listen. Write *c* or *g* to complete the word. 🎧 TR: 7.4

1. ___ity
2. ___oat
3. ___ood

4. hu___e
5. i___e / fa___e
6. do___ / hu___

C Look at the pictures and complete the crossword.

Across →   Down ↓

3.
1.

4.
2.

7.
5.

8.
6.

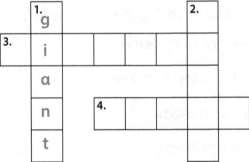

1. g
3. g i a n t
4.
5.
7.
6.
2.
8.

VALUE

Stay safe outside.

A **Which children are staying safe outside?** Look and circle.

B Write.

a helmet   water   lights

sun cream   the life guard   a life jacket

1. When you ride your bike at night, it's important to have _____ on your bike.

2. Be careful when you go running or exercise in hot weather. You must take _____ with you.

3. On hot, sunny days, always wear _____ on the beach.

4. If you like climbing in the mountains, it's very important to wear _____ .

5. Sailing is fun, but always put _____ on before you get on the boat.

6. Don't get in the swimming pool if your parents or _____ aren't there.

C **How do you stay safe outside?** Tick the things you do in Activity B.
Write one more thing you do.

_____

8 Exploring

Lesson 1 Vocabulary

A Look and write.

1. On Monday, we went to a _____ .

2. On Tuesday, we went to a _____ .

3. On Wednesday, we went to an _____ .

4. On Thursday, we went to a _____ .

5. On Friday, we went to a _____ .

6. On Saturday, we went to a _____ .

B Write.

| dinosaurs   funfair   museum   rides |
| ~~summer camp~~   water park   wildlife park |

1. I made lots of friends at ____summer camp____ .

2. I went on eight different _____ at the _____ .

3. I didn't swim much at the _____ .

4. I saw lots of animals at the _____ .

5. We learnt about _____ at the _____ .

C Listen. Write the place each speaker went to. 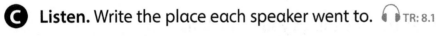 TR: 8.1

1. Ela went to an _____ .

2. Dev went to a _____ .

3. Leo went to _____ .

4. Rosa went to a _____ .

A Write.

Next week, my brother Andre ¹. _____ is going to visit _____ (visit) the new
wildlife park. His friend's parents ². _____ (take) his
friend and him. They ³. _____ (see) lots of lions and
hippos. But they ⁴. _____ (not / see) any penguins, my
favourite animal. I ⁵. _____ (not / go) to the wildlife park
with Andre. Mum, Dad and I ⁶. _____ (spend) the day
at a theme park! We ⁷. _____ (not / learn) about animals.
But I know I ⁸. _____ (have) lots of fun!

B Write what the children are going to do. Use *swim, sail, ride* or *go.*

Su-Jin	✓	✓	✗	✓
Feodor	✓	✗	✓	✗
Marcia	✗	✗	✓	✓

1. Su-Jin _____ is going to ride _____ a horse.

2. Feodor and Marcia _____ in the sea.

3. Feodor _____ on a lake, but he and Su-Jin
_____ canoeing.

4. Marcia and Feodor _____ a horse.

5. Su-Jin _____ in the sea.

6. Su-Jin and Marcia _____ on a lake.

C Write two things you are going to do after school and two things you aren't
going to do.

1. I'm going to _____ .

2. _____

3. I'm not _____ .

4. _____

A Write.

> chefs   circus   juggle   skills   stars   unicycle

1. a cycle with only one wheel _____

2. you see people doing amazing things here _____

3. people on TV, in films, etc. _____

4. these people work in the kitchen in restaurants _____

5. things you can do because you practise them _____

6. throw and catch three balls or other things at the same time _____

B **Read.** Write the word in the correct place in each line.

Cooking Camp

like

Do you ˇcooking? You're going to love Masterchef summer camp! In the **like**

mornings, you're to learn to cook with professional chefs and the young stars of **going**

the programme *Masterchef*! In the afternoons, you're going to have fun in the **TV**

Spanish countryside.

Circus Camp

Can you juggle? Well, you're going to learn! There are lots of fun to learn at a **skills**

circus camp in California, like walking on a rope and a unicycle. You're going to **riding**

sleep in a tent, climb trees and lots of friends. **make**

Wildlife Photography Camp

Go camping in the forests and mountains of Nilgiri in India, the animals that live **discover**

here and learn about fantastic photos at the same time! **taking**

C **Read again.** Write T (true) or F (false).

1. Children learn new skills at all three camps. _____

2. At Masterchef summer camp, the children cook all day. _____

3. The circus camp is in Spain. _____

4. At circus camp, you learn two skills. _____

5. You learn photography skills in California. _____

A **Listen and answer the questions.** 🎧 TR: 8.2

1. Is Elena going to stay in Poland this summer? _____ , she _____ .

2. Are Jack and Milo going to do their homework at the weekend? _____

3. Is Isaak going to swim at the beach this afternoon? _____

4. Are Lily and Eric going to go running? _____

B **Write questions and answers about the future.**

1. Arturo / learn to sail / ?
   Is Arturo going to learn to sail?

   Yes, _____he is_____ .

2. Inga and Tanja / walk in the mountains / ?

   _____

   Yes, _____ .

3. you and your brothers / sleep in a tent / ?

   _____

   No, _____ .

4. Emma / ride on a motorbike / ?

   _____

   No, _____ .

5. we / see shooting stars tonight / ?

   _____

   Yes, _____ .

6. I / see you at school next year / ?

   _____

   Yes, _____ .

C **Write questions and answers about the future.**

1. you _Are you going to have a big dinner?_ _____Yes, I am._____

2. your mum _____ _____

3. your friends _____ _____

4. your teacher _____ _____

A **Listen to how the *e* in *summer* is pronounced.** Circle the letters that make the same sound. 🎧 TR: 8.3

1. summer
2. Brazil
3. daughter
4. exercise
5. parents
6. crocodile
7. elephant
8. Poland

B **Listen.** How many schwa sounds can you hear in the underlined words? 🎧 TR: 8.4

1. Please send me a <u>letter</u>. ☐

2. Look at <u>the</u> <u>question</u> and <u>answer</u>. ☐

3. Don't eat on a <u>roller</u> <u>coaster</u>. ☐

4. She moved from <u>Canada</u> to <u>China</u>. ☐

5. I ate a <u>banana</u> at the <u>cinema</u>. ☐

6. <u>Crocodiles</u> are <u>amazing</u> <u>creatures</u>. ☐

C **Look.** Find and circle the words. Then write the words in the correct places.

Words with the schwa sound in the last syllable

1. A hot time of year → <u>summer</u>

2. A black-and-white animal → _____

3. Morocco's continent → _____

4. A warm top you wear in winter → _____

Words with two schwa sounds

1. A ride at a funfair → _____

2. Delicious yellow fruit → _____

3. A country in North America → _____

X	E	A	D	U	C	G	D	R	V	Y	D	J
Z	J	U	M	P	E	R	R	O	D	R	O	I
F	N	S	U	M	M	E	R	L	C	H	C	S
O	P	K	H	C	M	T	R	L	K	G	T	A
Z	Q	F	Y	W	V	Y	G	E	A	P	O	F
M	M	G	H	M	U	A	W	R	H	S	R	R
R	V	J	S	F	A	A	H	C	X	R	K	I
Y	R	G	V	N	R	Y	N	O	J	H	X	C
Q	E	C	C	E	H	N	B	A	N	A	N	A
Z	C	O	U	Q	S	L	U	S	J	J	W	U
Y	N	Z	E	B	R	A	R	T	Q	B	Q	G
P	E	M	Y	Z	B	A	D	E	L	L	W	W
U	C	A	N	A	D	A	S	R	N	H	M	S

VALUE
Plan your free time.

A **Look at Yolanda's calendar.** Write.

SUNDAY	MONDAY	TUESDAY	WEDNESDAY	THURSDAY	FRIDAY	SATURDAY
	1	2 6:00 p.m. basketball practice	3	4 7:30 p.m. guitar lesson	5	6 9:00 a.m. basketball game
7	8 science project	9 6:00 p.m. basketball practice	10 English test	11	12	13
14	15	16 6:00 p.m. basketball practice	17	18 7:30 p.m. guitar lesson	19 science test	20
21 11:00 a.m. basketball game	22 maths test	23 6:00 p.m. basketball practice	24	25	26 Sports Day at school	27 5:00 p.m. Beth's birthday party ☺
28	29	30 6:00 p.m. basketball practice	1	2 7:30 p.m. last guitar lesson	3	4 *Holiday!* ☺☺☺

1. What are Yolanda's hobbies?

2. What has Yolanda got on Wednesday, the 10th?

3. What has she got at the same time every week?

4. What other activities has she got that are **not** free time?

5. Is Yolanda good at planning her time?

B **Think about how you plan your free time.** Write.

1. How are you similar to and different from Yolanda?

2. Have you got a calendar like this?

C **Here is a calendar for next week.** Plan your free time! Write.

SUNDAY	MONDAY	TUESDAY	WEDNESDAY	THURSDAY	FRIDAY	SATURDAY

A **Find and circle the following things in the museum.** There are four words that aren't in the picture.

an ancient Maya city	a bus stop	a car park
an archaeologist	a café	a cinema
an art gallery	a canoe	a crying child

a dinosaur	a Pueblo building	a skyscraper
a laughing child	a ride	a sled
a lost child	a sculpture	a tent
a person climbing	a shooting star	

B **Cover the picture.** List as many things as you can remember from the museum.

_____ _____ _____ _____

_____ _____ _____ _____

_____ _____ _____ _____

_____ _____ _____ _____

The Comedy Wildlife Photography Awards

A **Listen.** Tick the words you hear. 🎧 TR: 8.5

☐ funniest	☐ do	☐ competitor
☐ animals	☐ laughing	☐ cheer
☐ favourite	☐ eleven	☐ fastest
☐ photos	☐ awards	☐ children

B **Complete the summary with the words you ticked in Activity A.**

There are many competitions where people can enjoy looking at photos of ¹·_____ .
The Comedy Wildlife Photography Awards is the first competition to show the ²·_____
wildlife photos. In this competition, famous people choose their ³·_____ funny photo.
The ⁴·_____ usually show animals that look as if they're ⁵·_____ or doing
funny things. There are seven ⁶·_____ and many chances to win!

C **Write T (true) or F (false).**

1. There are competitions for black-and-white photos of animals. _____

2. There aren't any competitions for photos of insects. _____

3. The Comedy Wildlife Photography Awards is the first competition
   for photos of funny animals. _____

4. The photos don't need to be funny. _____

5. Tom Sullam was one of the first winners of the competition. _____

6. The seven winners include the best photos of an underwater
   animal, an animal in the air and a video of an animal. _____

A Write two words in each sentence.

> canoeing + summer camp   dinosaur + museum
> rides + funfair   ~~roller coaster + theme park~~

1. We're going to go on the fastest
   __roller coaster__ at the __theme park__ .

3. We're going to go on lots of
   _____ at the _____ .

2. We're going to go _____ at
   _____ .

4. We're going to see a _____ at
   the _____ .

B Write the words.

1. We had a p_____ in the park. It was fun eating outside!

2. I made a new f_____ at summer camp. Her name is Leila.

3. My uncle let me ride on his m_____ when we stayed at his house.

4. Did you s_____ in the tent or in the house last night?

5. I liked swimming in the sea, but swimming in the l_____ was nicer.

6. They took the children to the water p_____ for the day. It was lots of fun.

C Write the past simple of the verbs.

Across →	Down ↓
2. see	1. play
7. sleep	2. ski
8. sit	3. is
9. make	4. get
10. help	5. climb
	6. walk

D Circle.

Hannah: Are you ¹·**doing** / **going** to do anything fun next month, Sara?

Sara: Yes, I ²·**am** / **did**. I'm going to ³·**stay** / **staying** with my grandparents.

Hannah: Cool! ⁴·**Are** / **Is** your big sister going to go with you?

Sara: No, she ⁵·**is** / **isn't**. She's going to travel with a school friend.

Hannah: So ⁶·**what** / **when** did you last see your grandparents?

Sara: ⁷·**Ago** / **Last** summer. They live far away, so we don't see them often. What about you? What are your plans?

Hannah: I ⁸·**go** / **went** on holiday already, in July.

Sara: Oh, really? Where ⁹·**did** / **do** you go?

Hannah: We went to Magic Mountain.

Sara: The theme park? Oh, wow! ¹⁰·**Where** / **Who** did you go with?

Hannah: I went with my mum, my dad and my brothers.

Sara: Did you ¹¹·**have** / **to have** fun?

Hannah: Yes, we ¹²·**did** / **going to**. It was amazing.

E Circle the word that has got a different sound. Listen and check. 🎧 TR: 8.6

1. -c-   centre   ice   sauce   cat

2. -c-   city   medicine   pencil   ancient

3. -g-   dangerous   page   tiger   vegetable

4. -g-   village   giraffe   girl   giant

Word List

Unit 1	Unit 2	Unit 3	Unit 4
blue	ants	almost	back
bottle	bat	a beard	calm
cup	busy	bird	a cold
flute	dolphins	curly hair	a cough
glass	fish	dark hair	down
milkshakes	fruit	die	flower
moon	hungry	fat	grade
noodles	kangaroo	light hair	ill
pancakes	lizard	metre	medicine
pasta	panda	a moustache	mouse
plate	parrot	round face	shoulder
salad	penguins	shark	shout
sandwiches	photo	straight hair	a sore neck
sauce	safe	sweetcorn	stomach
soup	shark	take (two hours)	tooth (teeth)
straw	wake up	tall	toothache
vegetables	whale	thin	worry

Unit 5	Unit 6	Unit 7	Unit 8
building	bear	cat	art gallery
bus stop	chair	city	camel
café	civilisation	eat outside	chef
car park	climb trees	explorer	circus
cinema	cry	giraffe	dinosaur
factory	cycle to school	go canoeing	funfair
hospital	invent	go on a roller coaster	juggle
lobster	laugh	goat	kangaroo
market	mystery	have a picnic	lemon
purple	need water	lose your way	museum
shopping centre	parents	make friends	pencil
skyscraper	sail	ride on a motorbike	ride
sports centre	scare	see a shooting star	sculpture
supermarket	statue	ski	skill
T-shirt	stay at home	sled	star
world	wait for the bus	sleep in a tent	summer camp
	walk to school	swim in a lake	theme park
			unicycle
			water park
			wildlife park

CREDITS